# Women's Intuition

## Realizing Your Worth

### by
### T. LaShaé

authorHOUSE™

1663 LIBERTY DRIVE, SUITE 200
BLOOMINGTON, INDIANA 47403
(800) 839-8640
WWW.AUTHORHOUSE.COM

First published by AuthorHouse 06/07/05

ISBN: 1-4208-5720-7 (sc)

Printed in the United States of America
Bloomington, Indiana

This book is printed on acid-free paper.

# Women's Intuition

Intuition is defined as fore knowledge, a gut reaction, a hunch, an innate knowledge or a sixth sense. People may not believe it but women really do have one. It can be known to some as a savior. It saves from heartache and from wasting our precious time on someone or something that was not worthy of it in the first place. Our intuition protects us from being made fools of. It protects our minds, our bodies, and our souls. A woman's intuition is her spirit speaking to her and revealing things that are going on now and the things that are to come. When your intuition speaks to you, listen. If you do not, it can hurt you. Literally. Think about it, you are minding your own business and going on with your daily routine. Bam! It hits you. It creeps up on you like a thief in the night. You come out of yourself and briefly become psychic. That is where the hurt comes into play. You have a weird pain in your stomach, which we call our "gut feeling". That will let us know that something is wrong. Normally, when we follow our intuition, it leads us to what we want to know and some times to things that we have already known all along. Men find it hard to believe that we do have a sixth sense. They think that it is comical that we would actually think up something like that. It is not too funny when what we believe or feel is right, huh?

Our intuition protects us from being mistreated, disrespected, misused, abused, and taken advantage of. If only we would take the time to listen to our intuitions, we can save ourselves from hurt and pain. We can dodge the blows to the face; we can walk away from being hurt, misused, and mistreated. By acknowledging our intuition, we will be able to protect ourselves from those people that bring heartache and pain. Listen to your intuition and pay attention to first impressions. Be aware of those you are surrounded by. Not everything that looks good is always good for you. There are times when your intuition may fade due to the intensity of the situation that you may be facing. You have to stay strong and focus on what is important. That is you. There is nothing in the world that is more important than you. When you have that "gut feeling", that something is not right, act on it. Do not try to figure out why. You already know. The proof is in actions.

Have enough courage to walk away from situations that you know are not good for you when things are not working out. There is nothing wrong with taking a little time out for you. Follow your intuitions and you will see what I am talking about. Once you have the answer, you will be able to realize your worth and know that you are worth far more than you are being offered.

# Why Not Want What is Best For You?

Why do we allow ourselves to be lied to? Why do we allow men to tell us what to do, where to go and how fast to get there? Why do we feel that just because we have been in a relationship with a man past six months that he has the right to talk to us crazy or disrespect us? Why? What is it? Do we feel that we are not worthy to be loved, respected or cherished and treated the way that we know we deserve to be treated? Let me tell you ladies, I have been there and I am not going back!

Whatever happed to those men that we women could brag about? Those that were not ashamed to say that they couldn't hang out because they had plans with their woman. Where are the romantic men? The man that will buy you flowers when it's not your birthday. Where are the men that call just to here your voice or just because they miss you? I have met so many guys that think that showing affection or loving his woman the right way is a sign of weakness. That's not true! What I think is weak is him not expressing the love that he has for his woman or anybody for that matter. If you can be excited and overzealous about the love for your mother or your sister then what is wrong with expressing the love for your wife or girlfriend? A man showing emotions is one of the greatest attributes of a real man.

I know that there has to be good men out there somewhere. Good men, where are you? Most of them are married or are close to being married. The ones that are not are either afraid of commitment or just, as they say, "sowing their royal oats". I don't know, it could be me or I might just be looking in the wrong places.

I know many men that live their lives rather scandalously. Multiple women, card playing, video games and a six pack of beer. That is their routine every day. I have a friend that calls me daily telling me about her no good man. "Paul has left the house once again to go play video games with his friends". Paul is a 29-year-old, sorry, video game playing, weed smoking, unemployed man. Can't keep a job cause he can never past the drug test and when he gets a job his anger management issues will not allow him to restrain himself from fighting at work.

While he is out living in his fantasy world, she is at home cooking, cleaning, taking care of the kids, and worrying about him. When she calls his cell phone, while he's out doing God knows what, he doesn't answer. The house could be on fire but, Paul doesn't care cause he is kickin' it. All he is thinking about is himself and the fun that he is having without her. If she's thinking about him and he's thinking about him, whose thinking about her? I told my friend a long time ago when she was complaining after one week of dating him that she should have cut him off then. Had she followed her intuitions she would not be dealing with a sorry, self-centered, pitiful excuse of a man. She has been spending years with a man that spends most of his day playing video games or watching basketball games at his friends' house. He comes home after he has spent all day with the fellas. He actually cooks dinner, runs bath water, and wants to make up for not making her the top priority of the day. What is the point of making up when tomorrow is going to be the same? Keep in mind that his day of hanging out ended at 12:30a.m. There is no way in this world that I would allow this man to come into my house and feel like he can touch me after neglecting me all day! He can't really look at me! I tell you what, he wouldn't be looking at me because he would not get in the house! If you cannot respect me enough to come in at a decent hour then I cannot respect you enough to let you in, playa!

What Paul did is not acceptable ladies! Hell, what my friend did was not acceptable either. She allowed a man that she knew was no good to come into her home and mooch off her and then she turns around and has the nerve to complain about it. She knew what she was getting herself into in the beginning. She obviously likes it because she is still dealing with him. It seems, sometimes, that women enjoy the company of a no good man. Women amaze me. Most women are attracted to those men that have no jobs and do not want anything out of life. They chose to pamper and spoil those types. For years, a woman will date the wrong man and be extra good to him, but when she finds the man that is right for her and treats her like a queen, she dogs him out. I am yet to understand that one. Women always talk about how they want to be happy and they are waiting for Mr. Right. How can that be said when we do not have the patience to wait for Mr. Right? Before Mr. Right comes along, we have already allowed every Tom, Dick, and Harry to invade our lives, our homes, our beds. We have already run through so many men that we do not have anything left to offer him. If we have already been deflowered by the world, what do we have left to offer Mr. Right? Why would we even waste our time? Everybody deserves a second chance, but before you need that second chance, you must first make the right decisions for your life.

Your intuition will tell you that this man that is in your face saying everything that you want to here is saying it just to get you out of your clothes.  Your intuition will tell you that this man that is buying you everything that you want and is not taking you any where or does not listen to what you have to say is not good for you. Your intuition will tell you to save yourself for marriage and wait for Mr. Right because you are worthy and he is worth it.  If you have already made the mistake of picking the wrong man and giving in to his every need, want and desire knowing that he is not worthy, do not beat yourself up about that.  It may have been because of a lack of knowledge due to a rocky upbringing or immaturity.  Only you have the power to make it right.  You have to be strong enough to say, "I deserve the best. In order for me to have the best, I have to want the best for myself. I have to carry myself the way that I want people to receive me." My friend allowed Paul to control her.  That is no way to live.  We are in control of every situation that we put ourselves in.  Whether it is good or bad, a man is going to treat you the way that you carry yourself.  We date with the possibility of marriage. If the crap that Paul tried to pull on my friend is pulled one time with me you are gone! It took me a while to get to that point, but be patient and it will be worth it. If a man puts a video game before me while we are dating, I can expect no more from him than a pack of tic-tacs as a gift for our first wedding anniversary.  What bothered me about my friends' relationship was the fact that she put up with Paul. That's my friend and I love her but, come on! Be real about the situation! They live together and have a child. How in the world can she expect to build a life with someone that does not want anything out of life? It is painfully obvious because he is 29 and does not have anything to call his own.  The apartment and the car belong to her. What kind of sense does that make.  I refuse to take care of a man that is not my child!  It is bad enough to have a man that is not there for her and not taking care of his responsibilities but its worst when he does not have a job and is living off you when he has a mama that can handle that for him!

If we would follow our intuitions, we probably would not fall for the guys that feed us these sad sob stories about how their past relationships or bad financial decisions messed up their lives and put them in the bad situations that they are in. We allow them to overpower us with their emotional distress as we become consumed by their hard times. That is how they get us. We are trapped like mice in mousetraps. What makes you think that we women are going to want you and want to be with you for the rest of our lives if you cannot deal with something as simple as your emotions? Be a man, suck it up, and move on! Do not allow a man to overpower your good judgment just because of his emotional issues.

Being a man means taking care of business. Not only when it's convenient to you but others as well. Being a man means taking charge and being in control mind, body and soul. Those men come far and few. I am not saying that all of them are the same but, the majority of them are. I'm sorry but the truth hurts. I am tired of meeting the sorry, needy men that are always nagging about what they want. "Baby, I need to be held" or "Baby, I need some more boxers" or "Baby, I need a massage" or even "Baby, I need you to fix my plate and hurry up and bring it to me." What about what we need? We work just as they do, sometimes even harder. Actually, if you think about it, we do work harder. It may not hold monetary value but it should. We take care of all of the needs of the children and the home, we take care of the needs of our man, and then we have to find time to take care of ourselves. They come home talking about being tired from working like you guys didn't get off at the same time. What does he think that you did all day? Just because his job might be a little more strenuous than yours doesn't mean that you might not have had a stressful and tiring day.

Just sit back, relax, and think for a moment. Look at your situation and think about how you feel. What is more important than your feelings? Nothing! Do not allow yourself to be fooled by the wolf in sheep clothing. They will try to use their conniving charm and slick wit to make you feel as if you are wrong but you have to be stronger and smarter than them and know that people will only get over on you if you allow them to.

It is funny how people can be so insensitive when feelings are involved. They will hurt you or do something to disrespect you and when you acknowledge what they did to hurt you, they get mad at you because you were smart enough to figure it out. What they do not realize is that the only reason why you were putting up with them is that you were blinded by loving them and saw no wrong in them because of the fact that you did love them. After a while, that gets old. Do not allow anybody to insult your intelligence! You are much smarter than that! People run into situations like that a lot in relationships today. If you really want to get technical about it, we run in to situations like that in everyday life.

# The Misuse of Your Intuition

If we utilized our intuition, as we should, we would not have to suffer from disrespect or mistreatment. We would not be confused by what love is. We would know the true meaning a never, ever have to question the word. We cannot let love blind us so that we confuse disrespect with love. I do not think that this kind of love has created that kind of love. If you are in a relationship with someone that is abusing you physically, mentally and emotionally, do not ever feel that you are the one with the problem. They have the problem. Nobody ever deserves to be mistreated. God has not made a person on this earth that has the right to mistreat you or make you feel like you are not worthy of love. If you are with someone and you feel that the person is not the one for you, don't take them down through there, let them go!

It is difficult for some of us to let go because we love so hard. We try to give people the benefit of the doubt only because we are in love with their potential. Their potential to be great lovers, friends and confidants. There is nothing wrong with seeing the good in people but do not let that cloud your judgment of them. You can actually get your signs that the person that you are involved with has the potential to be a batterer from their conversation, first couple of dates, even if horseplay gets too rough. A man that cares about you will not ever do anything to hurt you. Realize that no one on this earth has the right to mistreat you and get away with it. You are better than that! For you abusers and manipulators, think about how you would feel if someone mistreated your mother or your sister. You know that if someone were to ever mistreat them that

9

they would have hell to pay! If you really feel that way, then think of how you are making your woman feel. You call her out of her name. You don't take her anywhere as if you are ashamed of her. You lie to her and cheat on her. You hit her and then have the nerve to make up stories and try to convince yourself that you are such a good boyfriend that you can come home and she's supposed to please you. Stop for a moment and ask yourself, why? Why would she cook for you, why would she clean for you, why would she say nice things to you? You have to give to receive. Remember, you reap what you sow.

# Understand your Worth

Do we as women know fully what we are worth? Worth is defined as the quality that renders something desirable, useful, or valuable. Our desire comes from our grace, our elegance, and our sense of style. Our usefulness and our values show through dating, marriage, motherhood, and politics. Our sensitivity and vulnerability toward certain situations sometimes seems to confuse those who have no idea about the woman and her virtue. There is always a question about our role in society and things that we do and say just because we are women are often criticized and ridiculed. There was a time when women were to be seen and not heard. Thank God, those times have changed! The time has come for women to claim their places in this world. If we do not realize how precious we are, then who will? I do not under stand why some women feel that they need a man to define them. They search for love in the wrong places. It is impossible to love and be happy if you do not love yourself. No one should have to tell you that you are beautiful, worthy of love, or worthy of happiness. You should already know that. Understand your worth! Just because your mate in your previous relationship mistreated you and told you that no one would ever love, you does not mean that you are not worthy to be loved. That coming from the same man that did not care enough about him to brush his teeth everyday and get his hair cut regularly. This same man did not have enough respect for you or him to be discreet about the other woman that he was dating. Come on! You are worth more than petty conversation, an occasional date, and a quickie during lunch hour. You do not deserve the lies and deception. You definitely do not deserve to be the other woman! Why should you? You got it going on, maybe a lot more than the first woman does. Do not ever allow anybody to disrespect you like that!

My friend Julia called me telling me that she had been with this person for about ten years. She is a beautiful girl with a good job, has a beautiful little girl, and has so much going on for herself. This guy is the biggest thug that you ever want to meet. He thinks that he is God's gift to women because he is cute. I will give it to him, he is kind of handsome. The funny thing about him is that he really does not have it going on like he thinks. Other women have "blown his head up" so that he walks around as if he is Denzel Washington or someone famous like that. This guy is really a waste of her time. They have never been in a serious relationship; it was more of a sexual relationship. Ok, it was a sexual relationship. No strings attached. After a couple of years, she started falling in love with him. To him, it was just an "arrangement". You know how they get about arrangements. That's a chance for them to have their cake and eat it too. If you are an "arrangement", then he never has to do anything for you but fulfill your sexual desires.

Julia has now fallen head over heels for this man just because the sex is the bomb! She is having a hard time leaving him alone. I am just trying to understand why because their relationship is only based on sex. He has never done anything for her and has never gone out of his way to treat her the way a woman is supposed to be treated.

He does not take her out. He doesn't do anything special for her but, has the nerve to get mad when she does not acknowledge his existence. What in the world is so great about him that makes him feel like he is worthy of anybody's time. He is just taking advantage of her because she is sweet and will do what she can to help anybody out. If you allow them, they will play you! Understand that you are in control of how people treat you. If we allow them to mistreat us and call us out of our names then they are going to do just that. We have to be strong enough to let them know when enough is enough! Do you hate yourself that much? It is obvious that you do if you are going to allow him to treat you that way.

On the other hand, think about the woman that knows that she has it going on. No one can tell her anything bad about herself. No one can bring her down and steal her joy. She does not have to have a man in her life to be happy because she has occupied her time with activities that can benefit her in the future. It is so funny how we strong, independent women intimidate these men out here. When they see this woman coming, they get out of her way. They expect us to be whiny, overly sensitive, easily influenced, drama filled little girls. Oh no buddy, I don't think so? Our kindness is taken for weakness. Just because we smile, are sweet, willing to be there for you and will give you our last, does not mean that we are idiots and down for whatever. We are worth more than the materialistic things in this world!

We are wives, we are mothers and in this day in age we are the providers. We are responsible for teaching our sons how to be men because their fathers have chosen the world over the relationship with their child. We sacrifice everything to make sure that our children are taken care of and these men go out with their new wives or girlfriends trying to take credit for how good the child is doing, yet they were not at all involved in the child's upbringing. Some of them even think that paying child support means that they are playing their roles as parents. If you think that then you need to grow up! There is more to parenting than a check! You guys have to keep in mind that we single mothers are taking care of the children 24 hours a day and 7 days a week. That little $300's a month that you pay is for shelter. What about food, clothes, and the different necessities that they need in life? There are also those men out there that feel that if they are paying child support that is all they are supposed to do! If you really believe that, then you need to reconsider your thought of what a man should be.

We cannot continue to allow these people out here to try to run over us! Understand your worth! We are worth so much more than cars, clothes, jewelry and shoes. Those things are good to have but we real women do not see them as a necessity. We have to set goals for ourselves and have high standards when it comes to men and what we want. A man that really wants you will call you and pursue you. If you find yourself calling him all of the time, it is not because he does not like to talk on the phone; it is because he does not want to talk to you. It never fails. You go out one day and decide to be bold enough to approach a man because you are turned on by the way that he carries himself. Then, you decide that you want to get to know him better. Because women do not do this often, you really do not know how to approach him. You come on too strong, he gives you his number and when you call, he does not answer the phone. Hmm, I wonder why? He was not interested in you. Had he been interested in you, he would have approached you. The reason for that is because it does not take much for us women to fall for a guy. We tend to be more vulnerable when it comes to a handsome man with good conversation. For guys, that is a different story. With men, it depends on how they have been previously treated by another woman, the day of the week or where they are mentally in their lives. If you are looking to be in a relationship and you meet a man that has just got out of a relationship where he was hurt, you can hang that up. There are some of them out there that will take a chance. Come on guys, take a chance! There is always one bad apple that spoils the bunch. Do not let that be the reason that you miss your soul mate.

# Make Him Understand Your Worth

Robert made special reservations at Tina's favorite restaurant for her birthday. He promised that he would do that for her month's ago. The final NBA play off game happens to fall on Tina's birthday and Robert's friends have tickets. Tina has been made aware that his friends have tickets and she hasn't thought twice about them because she knows that her man is not going to break their plans. Robert actually considers going to the basketball game. He actually has the nerve to ask Tina if it's ok to go seeing as though he has never been to a NBA playoff game. After arguing with her and telling her how selfish she is for not wanting him to go, Robert goes to the game anyway. It's so funny how men try to flip the script when they want things to go their way. The only reason why he started the argument was to have a reason to leave. When he comes home, he is not going to be focused on the fact that he broke the plans that you all had but his excuse for leaving will be because you started the argument. What he let her know at that very moment that he left was that a basketball game was worth more than she was. We women look into things a little deeper than men do. He called her selfish to play on her emotions and make her feel like she was wrong. He is not looking at the fact that he lied to her and broke his promise to her. It never fails. He does something wrong and you point out what he did wrong. Instead of him being a man and owning up to what he did, he gets mad at you for being smart enough to figure out what he did.

There are many men out there walking in Robert's shoes. If you want to be selfish, be selfish by yourself! It is as simple as that!

Be realistic. You are in a relationship with someone. You don't spend any time with that person. You put things such as basketball, football, the play station and your boys before them. Sometimes, you even break bad and go out by yourself so that you can "cool off" or chill. Yeah right! You are doing everything in this relationship by yourself. Well, not everything because from time to time we are good for sex. So if you are kickin' it by yourself, why are you in a relationship? Let me stop and give men the benefit of the doubt for a moment because they will only do what we allow them to do. If we allow men like Robert to disrespect us, play on our emotions and put basketball games before us, maybe we might need to reevaluate ourselves. Had Tina listened to her intuitions, she would have been able to notice along time ago that her husband was selfish. She has always known that it was his way or no way at all. Now, she wants to get mad. There is no need for her to be upset because when she realized that he was that way, she talked to herself and told herself that she would be able to deal with it. If you chose to deal with it, do just that. If you know that you are not strong enough to handle a man like that and you know that you are worthy of more, then leave when you get your first signs. Just as simple as that.

The way that we are treated is totally up to us. If a man sees that you carry yourself the way that a lady should then he will come to you correct. If you are walking through the mall dressed nice, hair done, walking confidently, 9 times out of 10 a man is not going to approach you the wrong way. He might not approach you because confident, strong women intimidate men. On the other hand, if you are at the mall sporting your best hoochie gear, your hips hanging out and your breast bulging from your shirt, what do you expect? Respect is not just given freely you have to earn it. You earn it by first respecting yourself. Carry yourself like you know that you are everything and the world is yours. Understand that God created you and he chose you to bring life into this world. That's an honor. Do not ever let anyone tell you that you are not, because you are. We deserve a lot more than what we are offered.

If a man does not love you for who you are, he does not love you at all. If he is being cordial or doing a few things to show interest, that does not mean that he loves you. He is in love with either a fantasy or something special that you are doing for him. Because of that false sense of love, we allow people to control our lives. They control the way that we think, the way that we live and the way that we love. I do not know why we allow it! That is ridiculous! That's not what a relationship is all about. People complicate things when it's not even necessary to make them feel like they are in control. Are you really happy with having a leash on your significant other? Is it right to have an attitude like that with someone that you are planning to spend the rest of your life with? Your answer to those questions should be NO! Only a person with low self-esteem, no self-respect, and low sense of pride would be silly and childish enough to say yes.

Lack of parenting has a lot to do with how some people treat each other. If a person is not shown love and affection growing up, how can you expect them to show it to you? If a person has never seen their parents hug each other, kiss each other, or even say a kind word to one another, they definitely do not know what to do with you.

# Respect Yourself!

How can you expect someone to respect you if you do not respect yourself? Respecting yourself means taking care of you physically, mentally, and emotionally. You respect yourself physically by keeping up your appearance. I guarantee that you find so much joy and happiness in doing something to enhance your beauty. Mentally, we have to know ourselves that we are beautiful and worthy of everything that this world has to offer. We allow people to make us feel that we are ugly and unattractive with both mental and emotional abuse or by disrespecting us. We let our guards down and put all of our trust, love and faith in people and give them power over us. What we have to realize is that no one has power but God, so when people start moving mountains then I'll bow down. It took marriage and a lot of hard times and struggles for me to gain the personal relationship with God that I should have already had. That is when I really learned to respect myself. My intuitions told me that this man and I were marrying each other for the wrong reasons. My intuitions told me that this man did not love me. My false sense of love had convinced me that he was the one because he talked the good talk and walked the good walk. I have always served the Lord and always known that he is real but I did not fully understand his power and grace until me and my husband separated. I felt that I didn't have anybody. I knew that I had my mom but I didn't want to worry her with my problems. I felt so bad about myself. It was April of 2002. I was on the verge of losing my job, my house and my mind. I didn't feel that I was worthy of anything. That's when the Lord started working with me. I started to remember what I had been taught in the church growing up. I started to pray and ask the Lord to bless me with the wisdom and knowledge that I needed to fight the devil and get out of this situation that I had put myself into. Gaining a personal relationship with God turned my whole world around. For a long time I looked towards man for happiness. I never knew happiness until I allowed God to come into my life. Why look for man to make you happy when you have a man in your life that is promised to love you forever? When I need someone to talk to, I talk to the Lord. When I am weak, he strengthens me. When I am sick, he heals me. When I am weary, he comforts me. What more can you ask for?

I found a happiness that I had never known. I realized that I didn't have to have a man or the many treasures of the world to be happy. I found joy in making myself happy. Going shopping, getting my hair done or getting my nails done made me happy. We have to do things to make ourselves happy. How can we make somebody else happy if we are not happy with ourselves?

My friend Ronald was dating this girl named Helen. Ronald and Helen graduated from college together. After graduation, they had a baby and got married. Helen was a tall, beautiful woman with long jet black hair that came a little past her shoulders. She was very outgoing and found joy in everything that she came across. Ronald, however, was a really cool guy but, he had very low self-esteem. He was handsome. He was a clean cut guy. He always dressed nice and kept himself up. He had the most beautiful smile. Tall dark and handsome! Before they got together, Ronald dated a girl in college that he was madly in love with. Her name was Victoria. We are not really sure what happened between them but, she broke up with him. That really broke his heart. When he and Helen started dating, he would joke around with her, so he says, comparing her to Victoria and he would put down every thing that she did. She did not pay much attention to it because she loved him. When they finally got married, he changed for the worst. Helen always went out of her way to make this man happy and it seemed that there was nothing that she could do to make him happy. She noticed that when he was around other people he was always happy. When they would be alone, he acted like he hated her. He would tell her all of the time that he didn't love her and that the only reason why they got married was because they had a baby together. He wouldn't take her any where. He went out every night and would not come back until morning. Nobody could understand why he was treating her like that. You see, Ronald was treating her like that because he was unhappy. He never fully got over the fact that he was no longer with Victoria. He knew that Helen was a good woman but, that is not the woman that he wanted. Instead of being honest with Helen, he made her miserable. Instead of her using her brain and leaving, she stayed because she loved him. Misery loves company. For a while they both had gotten comfortable with in their situation. She did not believe in divorce and he did not want to leave because although they were having problems, none of the outside world knew that and he wanted everybody to think that everything was ok. She allowed him to degrade and disrespect her for 2 years before she realized her worth. All it took was for Helen to get fed up and put her foot down. She made him aware that she was not going to take his crap anymore. She was not used to feeling down and depressed. She was not used to being disrespected like that. She realized that he was taking her down through there and she was not going to put up with it any more. She packed his stuff and sent him back to his mother. If he wants to be miserable, why not be miserable by his self and away from her? That would make it easier on both of them. Helen let that go on for 2 years. She was miserable, unhappy and alone. Ladies, don't walk in Helen's shoes! She was badly taken advantage of because she loved him. It is ok to love but do not let love make a fool out of you. It took her 2 years to finally realize that he did not love her. If she would have been honest with herself and her situation and observed her relationship from the beginning, she would have known how he felt about her. It only takes a couple of months to know whether or not somebody is into you and really cares about you. Not about what you have and what you can do for them. They care about you and how you feel. What you are going through or have already been through. Ronald played Helen because he knew that she had low self-esteem. He knew that if she allowed him to disrespect her in the beginning and let him get away with it that he could continue to do it because she didn't respect herself. Respect yourself!! Show that man that you love you and he will respect and love you. People will only do what you allow them to do.

# Don't Be A Fool For Love!

How can we expect someone to love us when we do not love ourselves? If we do not love ourselves then we are making it harder for someone else to love us. We will be unhappy, always unsatisfied and we might even run away the one person that truly loves us. We have to re-evaluate our lives and try to figure out what it was that made us unhappy in the first place. Once you can do that, you will be free to love without any problems or stipulations. There is always that one person that can mess it up for everybody. You know that person that you fell so madly in love with that did not share the same love for you as you did them. Instead of them being honest with you and letting you know that they did not love you the same, they decide to take advantage of the situation. After awhile they turn into someone else. You think to yourself, "This is not the man that you fell in love with!" You become aware of this but yet you still stay with him because you love him. There is no need for him to be a punk about it. He could just be a man and let you know that he does not think that you are the one for him. He should let you know that before you get too deep into the relationship. That is too much like right. You try to do everything that you can to make this man fall back in love with you only to realize that you will be wasting your time because he did not love you in the first place. That is devastating! In the end, you have dedicated most of your time trying to rekindle something that never was. That love that you had for him goes from love to confusion, confusion to anger, anger to bitterness and bitterness to hatred. You become a woman scorned. This is where loving yourself comes in. If you love yourself, something like this can never happen to you. You cry for a minute and move on. Do you know why it will never happen to you? You are better than that! Someone close to you can tell you that until they are blue in the face but it means nothing until you start to believe it for yourself. We cannot allow men to think that they are the reason why we exist. So what, you guys broke up? That was his lost! If you always keep your guard up and pay attention to what he says and how he acts the signs will be there for you. I guarantee that they are there. If you are a very observant person, you will be able to figure out the intentions of a man through his conversation. If you are dating someone that is always unhappy, mad at the world, says that he doesn't smile but, smiles at people other than you or says that he is always mean but, when he gets around his friends or family he is just a cool and happy go lucky guy then you can't expect to get too far with that guy. He is either upset about a past relationship where he was hurt and he does not know how to get over that or he just does not like you. The reason why he is with you is because you are doing something for him or he wants his boys to think that he is the man because he treats his girlfriend like a child and she lets him. I don't know, some crap like that. You know how they do. Don't be fooled by his charm and the things that he is doing for you. He really isn't doing it for you. It is all for show. To him, you are just a trophy and you are allowing him to put you on display. Just because you are longing to be in love does not mean that you have to fall in love with the first person that gives you the attention that you are seeking. Men play on that. Of course, they would if you are telling them all of your business. When you first meet them, you tell them about how your last boyfriend dogged you out and you let them know what you are looking for in a man. If you observe the beginning of your relationship, you will see that he is exhibiting all of the traits of the man that you described. Just watch, you will find out what he is about much sooner than you expected.

It is truly amazing how people allow love to make fools of them. Let us take Jack and Rachel for example. Jack and Rachel met while working at a local department store. At the time, Jack was already dating Tonya, the lead cashier. Rachel was unaware of their relationship because she never saw them together and they acted as if they did not know each other. Rachel never thought that she would have a chance until Tonya came to work and announced that she found another job and would be leaving in a couple of days. That was Jack's opportunity to move in. Rachel had been attracted to Jack since the first day that he started working there. Jack was 6'5 muscular build and Rachel's eye candy. All it took was a couple of cheap dates at McDonald's for Rachel to fall in love with him. Rachel was a very sweet girl, somewhat intimidating because of her size. She came from a wealthy family, was about to graduate from college, and move into her new home. Jack, still at home with his mother, barely legal and making $4.45 an hour. He had no drive, no ambition and the only thing that meant anything to him was his new Play station games and basketball. Jack and Rachel really liked each other but the chemistry was not there. After a couple of months of dating, Jack moved in with Rachel. Rachel knew exactly how she felt about him but she was not quite sure of how he felt. The only thing that Jack had on his mind was being free of his nagging mother. He did not pay attention to Rachel at all. He treated her more like a roommate than a girlfriend. Rachel did not realize that he only saw her as a way out. She did everything for him. She offered this man her home, her car, her heart but that was not good enough for him. He used her so badly and she allowed him to. She allowed this man to cloud her judgment just because she thought that she was in love. She never realized that she was in love with a lie. During the first couple of months of him living there, he put her so far in debt. Instead of Rachel stepping up, putting her foot down, and demanding the respect that she deserved, for months, she let him run all over her. Finally, before he totally sent her to the poor house, she grew a brain and put her foot down. Personally, I would have left him where he stood. Why let a man that does not own anything but his clothes put you through all of that financial strain? That is not love! If he loved her, he would not have used her like that. That is not even the half of their fiasco. Rachel was not as strong as she thought that she was. Jack continued to make a fool out of her. He was showing her everyday that he did not want to be with her. He was trying to figure out everyday how to break up with her and she still did not get the point. He would pack up all of his belongings and just leave without an explanation. He was not even smart enough to leave after an argument; he would wait until they would make up and then leave. How stupid is that? However, after all of that, she still loved this man. Rachel allowed this man to make a fool out of her and for what? Was it for companionship? She allowed a man that had nothing going on for him to come into her life and make a complete fool out of her. A person with common sense would have noticed that the only reason why he was with her for her material possessions. He saw her as his opportunity to live the life of a wealthy man and not have to work for it. There is nothing wrong with doing things the way that Rachel did, but Rachel messed up by not having control of her life and using love as an excuse for her mess-ups. If he really did love her, he would have worked with her instead of against her.. All Rachel had to do was put her foot down and let him know what she would take and what she was not going to take. Be smart about your relationships and don't be a fool for love.

We often get confused about what love is. Falling in love is very simple. You can fall in love with someone that is there for you and gives you the attention that you need whether it be a joyous occasion or a time when things are not going too well. There is a difference between loving someone and being in love. You love someone that is there for you no matter what. Being in love is like a child eating candy for the first time. It is sweet and the feeling lasts forever. It is impossible to say that you are in love with someone and at the first sign of trouble, you turn your back on them. It's deeper than that. If you truly love someone, no one would ever have to question you about it. You guys would share the same intimate stare when looking at each other. Every time that you are together would be just like the first time you met. Him holding your hand would make you feel like a schoolgirl enjoying time with her first boyfriend on the playground.

You will know that you have been bitten by the love bug because whenever he is not with you the thought of him overwhelms you so that you can hardly catch your breath. It drives me crazy to know that there are actually women out there that know that their man is misusing the word love and they still stick by them and defend them as if it is ok. The man can be gone all day, with no phone call, of course. She can allow him to come home after midnight. He apologizes for being out all day and thinks that I love you is going to make everything better. That woman thinks that he is sorry because he said that he loves her. If that is love, I do not want any. How can he love her and he does not even care about her. They use the word love to throw you off sometimes. Pay attention to your relationship. For the woman that is questioning whether her man loves her, watch your man.  If you guys get into it every day about the same issues or if he constantly messes up to make up, you have your answer. Do not stay with a man out of obligation.  You are better than that. What is the obligation? Nothing!  "He is my baby's daddy and I love him!" And?  So what?  What the hell does that mean?  Are we really that blinded by love (or the thought of being in love) that we would compromise our whole lives for it?  Even when it's a lie? Sadly, I have to say that some of us do.  He lives with you but he is never there.  He goes out but not with you.  he picks fights with you so that he can have a reason to leave.  He does not want to be the one to blame for the relationship not working so he puts everything on you.  Do not be naïve and allow these men to play you. Show them that you are smart enough to peep out the game before they play it.  Remember, a person that does not stand for nothing falls for anything.

# Don't Play Me!

Women, wake up! It is a new day. I am so sick and tired of you weak women out here that are giving us strong women a bad name. Those women that are walking around whining and crying over a man that is not in love with them. Just because you are in love with somebody that does not obligate them to love you back. Don't be distraught and give up because that man doesn't love you! There are too many men in this world to be crying over one. If it does not work out with the one that you are with, cry a little bit and take your behind shopping or do something special for yourself. That is the first stage of moving on. Do something for yourself that makes you happy. There is no one in this world that can make you happier than yourself.

There is nothing that aggravates me more than a woman that is defending a "no good" man. Every time you talk to her she is crying about how bad he treats her or how he never takes her anywhere but, when you give your advice about the situation she will defend him. That man can be beating her and she will defend him to the end. What is the point of the conversation? I see it like this, if you are going to defend him, whatever it is that he is doing to you or not doing for you, keep it to yourself! Obviously you like it because you are still there. Why are you going to waste your time and the time of the friend that you are sharing your problems with? If you have a headache, you take Tylenol. If you have menstrual cramps, you take Midol. If you have a man that cannot be there for you when you need him, you take your ass on and find a man that will. Don't go out and find love, let love find you.

Love, love, love! That's all we want! That's all we need! Everybody wants it and everybody deserves it but, don't be a fool getting it. We sometimes do stupid things when we are in love. I'm all for helping somebody that is in need but, I am not going to get evicted or get a car repossessed for a man. You are about to lose your house to help him and his wife save theirs. Oh yes, it's true! See you are the other woman because he's not going to do his number one woman like that. Sorry buddy, I am not the one. If you have a man that is treating you like crap when you are doing everything that he wants you to do, you better believe that he has another woman. He can't wine and dine you!

His main woman needs a new wardrobe. The woman that he is really in love with is that strong woman that does not put with his mess. The only reason why he has you around is that it is convenient to him. There are not a lot of people in this world that will quickly turn down free stuff. I know women that go all out of the way to make the man that they are with happy and he is literally not doing anything for them. Nothing! From time to time, he may say something sweet to her or make promises that he and she knows that he is not going to keep. He is not there for her like she is there for him because he obviously does not love her like she loves him. That is pitiful! There is not anything wrong with him not loving her because not everybody that you meet is going to feel the same way about you that you do them but, do not take advantage of their kindness or lead them on. I have no sympathy for those people that are taken advantage of because obviously they like it. If you did not like it, you would not be there. No person in their right mind is going to allow their spouse or anyone for that matter to disrespect or mistreat them. If you are not going to allow a stranger to mistreat you, why is it ok for your spouse to do it? We are in control of everything that goes on in our lives. We have to carry ourselves the way that we expect people to perceive us as. It is funny how we sometimes get confused when it comes to love and the baby's daddy. If you have a baby's daddy that is not doing anything for your child and do not have a job, do not won't a job and really can't get a job because it's not guaranteed that he will pass the drug test, he does not need to be a part of your life. What in the world can this man do for you that you can't do for yourself? You may not realize it but you have it going on. You have a good job that allows you to pay your bill and get your children whatever their hearts desire. Why is it that every month it's time to pay your bills, you have no money? Hmm, I wonder why? You have gone out of your way for that low down, good for nothing, sorry excuse for a man. Whatever it was that he needed the money for, you were there with no problem. No questions asked. Think about this. Whenever you need something for yourself or for the kids you always get the old "Awe, I don't have it right now". The funny thing about that response is that you accept that. He knows you and he knows that when he asks you to do something, you are going to go all out for him, but he obviously doesn't want anything out of life so what makes you think that he wants you? A man that can't keep a job can't keep a woman.

# Looking For Love?

Love is one thing that everybody wants but no one can seem to find. There are so many people that have been hurt by love that they won't even give it a chance. It is so silly to say that that you are hurt by love because love and hurt don't mix. Love does not hurt. It is people that hurt. Just say that you are in a relationship with someone and you fall in love with them. You put your all into the relationship and you show them not only by words but actions that you love them. If the love that you are showing is not returned then maybe you are not with the right for them and they you. Don't take it personal! You and that person were probably not meant to be together. There is nothing wrong with that. It happens like that sometimes. Every relationship that you are in is not always going to be the way that you want it to be. That is just a part of life. Yes! Disappointment happens to be a part of life. Some people act as if it is new to them. There are going to be times in our lives when things are not going to go right but we have to be strong enough to overcome the many obstacles that come our way.

If you are really looking for love and happiness, treat people the way that you want to be treated. The way that you treat people, believe it or not, really can have a major affect on your life. If you are truly, a God fearing person you know what I am talking about. I have seen so many friends and family go through unheard of things and they can't understand why. Like my grandmother used to say, "God don't like ugly!" If you are mistreating somebody by words, not being there for them or what ever it may be and you think that you are getting away with it, you are dead wrong. Believe me, somebody's watching! Think for a minute. You are being nice to a certain group of people. You do things for people but then you bitch and complain about it. You are rude and nasty to for no apparent reason and you can't understand why things are not going right in your life! When you are in certain situations ask yourself, "What would Jesus do?" "Would he have talked to that person like that?" "Would he have been rude and nasty?" No. There are a lot of people out here that think just because they are doing a couple things right in their lives that it's ok. They think that they are doing just enough to get to heaven but that is not the case. Before you open your mouth, think about how you would feel about the statement that you are about to make. You are not the only person in this world that has gone through something. The person that you are talking crazy to or mistreating is probably going through something or has been through something so dramatic that they can't handle the little criticism that you are giving them. Treat people the way that you want to be treated and your blessing will be coming in so quickly that you will not be able to count them on your fingers.

How can you really expect to fall in love when all you do is spend most of your time thinking about how deeply somebody hurt you? While you are dwelling on the past you could be missing out on the one true love of your life. There are so many people out here that talk about they have never been in love because it is hard to find somebody. That is not true. Normally, we tend to fall in love with people that we know don't love us and by the time we find somebody that truly loves us, we are so scorned by the previous person that we treat the one who loves us like crap. We are always willing to take chances with someone that gives us bad signs in the beginning and that lets us know that they are not the one for us but, when the one actually comes along they we treated like doormats and walked all over and under appreciated. Why wait for love? You know that love is what you are seeking so why is it that when you find it you act like a child and don't know what to do with it? With some people it is a game and a vicious cycle that they continue to go in. All of that is not necessary. Live life, love and be happy. That is all that it is about.

# When a Woman's Fed Up

Carrie had taken all that she could take. Ryan was constantly calling her out of her name and making her feel like she was not worth of anything. He beat her everyday over little things. Not folding his clothes correctly or cooking his food the way that he thought that she should. He would think that having sex with her was doing her a favor or doing something special for her. Carrie was a beautiful girl, had a wonderful job, and had a lot going on for herself. She had just completed 4 years of college, got her Master's degree in Psychology but, something was missing. She could not understand why the man that she loved so much was treating her like she was nothing. She had done everything for this man. She put him through school. Her dad hooked him up with the job that he had. She bought him the car that he is driving his other women around in. She did everything for this man and he could never stop to say thank you. One day, Carrie sat down and weighed her pros and cons. She realized that she had more positive things going on in her life than negative. The only negative thing in her life that was standing in the way of her happiness was that no good man in her life. She finally put her foot down and kicked him to the curb. Her women's intuition spoke to her. It made her realize that she did have to put up with this man. He was not attached to her at the hip. She did what she had to do. Why is it wrong for you to hurt the feelings of someone that hurts you on the regular? There has to come a time in our lives when we realize the true value of our being. It is unnecessary for a man to feel that in order to get our attention he has to mistreat us. All it takes is a little love and attention and we will do almost anything for you. There is no reason in the world why we women should be putting up with this kind of mess from any man. There are too many men in this world for us to be settling for the first man that looks good or gives us good conversation. "Every thing that looks good is not always good for you." That is what my grandma used to tell us. That is so true.

It is hard for me to understand how a woman can be in a relationship with a man that is not good to her. What really gets me is that she takes time out of her day to complain about how he is treating her. When doing that, she is making him out to be more important than he really is. Your intuition should tell you that if you are not happy leave. I know, that is easier said than done, right? Wrong! Get up off your lazy butt, stop feeling sorry for yourself, and realize your worth. A man can rob you of your material possessions but he can never steal your joy. He can never rob you of your spirit or your peace of mind. It will be of no help to you for the people around you to know what you are worth if you do not know for yourself. If you do not know, you will be one more lost soul in the world.

When a woman is fed up, there is nothing that you say to change her mind. You can beg, plead, buy the things that she likes, and still get nothing. After we have given our all to someone that is it. No turning back. Do not stick around to constantly be hurt or stabbed in the back. Why? There are too many things going on in this world for us to dwell on unnecessary things. For example, the past. There are so many people in the world that live everyday in the past. They have a hard time moving on with their lives because of something bad that they have experienced. Whether it be a bad relationship, a mistake that a friend or family member made, that, by the way, may not have been intentional but they are so comfortable living in the past that they cannot see past it. Disappointment is a part of life. You go through it and move on. You cannot dwell on it because it will always be there. The really sad thing about them is that they want to be loved. Everybody wants that. What is sad is that when someone comes into their lives that loves them the way that they want to be loved, they have a hard accepting it. They have been so secluded in their comfort zone of hurt and pain that they do not know how to respond to love. Sometimes it is ok to make an exception for those people but there is only so much that you can take. Understand where they are coming from but do not be a fool. If allowed, they will play you.

The worst person to be, when dealing with a person that lives in the past, is one of the people that happened to hurt that person. I see it like this, you have people in your life that you trust and associate with, and you have people that you do not associate with. It is just as simple as that. What is the point of allowing someone that hurt you back into your life, giving them a second chance, just to throw what they did to you back in their face? If you are going to do that then there is no need to deal with the person because it is obvious that you have not gotten over whatever it is that they did to you. If you have allowed this person the opportunity to have a second chance, give it to them. Do not dwell on their past mistakes because that might just be the one that will be there for you when you least expect it.

# Listen to your intuition!

Women, listen to your intuition! Your intuition makes you aware of people and the things around you. It allows you to decipher whether or not someone is in your life for your good or your bad. Many women misconstrue what the women's intuition is all about. For every question that you ask, the first thought about that question was the answer that you were seeking. No need to ask around. This chapter is directed mainly toward you women who totally ignore your intuition. You women who walk around like a chicken with it's head cut off trying to figure out why things do not work out for you. These are the women that would rather listen to the advise of someone less fortunate than them instead of going with their first minds. You know, I have to get on those women that lost good men because of not following their intuition or pure stupidity. Whether he is your husband, a boyfriend, or the father of your children. I know that there are probably many women out here that have run their husbands off because they listened to their friends (that have never been married) rather than their intuitions or their husbands for that matter. Normally, they use excuses like "he works too much", or "he does not show me enough attention". If you know that there are bills that need to be paid and you are not making enough money to pay them, why would you get mad because your man chooses to get two jobs to support the family? Come on! Doesn't take a rocket scientist to see that. Obviously, you need to get a hobby. For you women out there that will allow a woman (that does not have a man or worst your family) to run your good man away, grow a brain and think for yourself. First, think about how your significant other is treating you. Nine times out of ten, the person that you are receiving advise from is not getting nearly as much of attention from her mate ( that's if she has one at all) than you are. Second, this person may just be jealous of you and is blowing little things in your relationship way out of proportion. Third, always do what is best for you. You will always know deep down whether the person that you are involved with is right for you.

This is the greatest part of this chapter. Listen up women. Pay close attention. This subject is going to be quite touchy but we are all adults, I think you can handle it. Let us now detour to the subject of the baby momma and how some of you (and you know who you are) can't spell intuition and wouldn't know what it was if it kicked you in the behind. I cannot believe some of the women in the world. What greater pain is there than to know that the father of your child is not there for your baby? It is hard to be a mother that knows that the father of her child is aware of his responsibilities and is not trying to have anything to do with their child. It is even harder to believe that there are actually women out here that have the audacity to deny a man the right to see his child when she knows that he will be there. Everybody that knows the father and interacts with him knows that he is all about taking care of his child. She knows that he will take of his child. The only reason why she is denying him visitation is because she is mad at the fact that he does not want to be with her. There are more people in situations like that, than you will ever know. There is this woman that I know. We will call her Jeanette. She did not have a lot going for herself. She was hopping in and out of one relationship to another searching for the perfect man. She would meet these guys (that she knew were no good) that would take advantage of her and leave her with empty promises. She decided that she was not going to allow another man to hurt her, as she had been hurt in the past. She made a wise choice to do that but she went about it the wrong way. See, one day Jeanette met a wonderful man named Charles. Charles was a laid back, intellectual who had not really experienced as much of life as Jeanette had. He was not the typical man. He was not into the normal lewd or whorish acts that most men practice in their spare time. He respected himself, the woman that he was with, as well as every individual person around him. Charles had doubts about a relationship with this woman because of her sorted past but he could not resist because there was something that drew him to her. He worshiped the ground that she walked on. She knew that they did not have a lot in common but he was a good man, what did she have to lose. Everything was good between them before she started running her mouth. Whenever she and Charles would have a fight, she would run and tell her friends. Of course, she would exaggerate most of her stories to make him look like the bad guy. What her friends did not know is that Jeanette caused most of their arguments because of her infidelity. She thought that she could sleep around on him, he find out and not say anything. Yeah right. Charles is in a dilemma because he loves this woman. He knows that he can't trust her but he stays with her. Jeanette even broke bad and had a child on him and he still stayed with her. He was so committed to her and the relationship that he stayed with her and was still there for her and child. Here comes the real drama. Jeanette gets pregnant again. This time, the baby belonged to Charles. After their baby was born, she totally flipped the script. She treated him as though he was the one that cheated on her and had done her wrong. Her actions blew him away. Charles could not believe that he spent years with woman and put up with infidelity, disloyalty, and total disrespect just for this woman to mistreat him like this. He felt as though everything that he did for her was in vain. Although she continued to mistreat him and bad talk him to her family, he still stuck around. He stayed with her and took care of his child as well as the child that she had with someone else. If you ask me, this girl is really living the life. Had she been dealing with the typical man, he would have already kicked her to the curb or worst.

## About the Author

LaShaé was born in Memphis, TN. She is a hard working, single mother of two. She became inspired to write while trying to figure out how to deal with her emotions from a traumatic and painful childhood. She has had several poems published with the American Poets Society and the Circle of Poets. Her dream is to one day have one of her books be a part of Oprah's book club.

www.ingramcontent.com/pod-product-compliance
Lightning Source LLC
Chambersburg PA
CBHW050349290526
45785CB00006B/2704